Pete's Picnic

by Steve Jacobson
illustrated by Angela Adams

Practice Decodable 57

McGraw Hill Education

Bothell, WA • Chicago, IL • Columbus, OH • New York, NY

MHEonline.com

Send all inquiries to:
McGraw-Hill Education
8787 Orion Place
Columbus, OH 43240

ISBN: 978-0-02-138974-2
MHID: 0-02-138974-8

Printed in China.

8 9 10 11 12 DSS 27 26 25 24 23

"We can go on a picnic or to the park," Mom told Pete.

"Let's go on a picnic," Pete said.
"I'll make sandwiches."

Pete's sandwich was big.
Mom's sandwich was small.

“I’ll make these equal,” said Pete.

He spent lots of time making the sandwiches even.

"I have a secret," said Mom.
"The weather turned wet."

"Still, we will have a picnic," she said.

They did. It was the best picnic!